You're God's Girl!

PRAYER JOURNAL

HARVEST HOUSE PUBLISHERS
EUGENE, OREGON

Cover design and illustration by Julia Ryan

Cover image © Mikhaylova Liubov / Shutterstock

Interior design by Rockwell Davis

HARVEST KIDS is a trademark of The Hawkins Children's LLC. Harvest House Publishers, Inc., is the exclusive licensee of the trademark HARVEST KIDS.

You're God's Girl! Prayer Journal
Copyright © 2021 by Jonathan Pitts
Published by Harvest House Publishers
Eugene, Oregon 97408
www.harvesthousepublishers.com

ISBN 978-0-7369-8328-0 (hardcover)

Printed in China

23 24 25 26 27 28 / RDS-RD / 10 9 8 7 6 5 4 3

Welcome to Your Prayer Journal!

You know that feeling you get when you're hanging out with your best friend and you're having so much fun? You can have the same feeling when you spend time with God. He wants to be the friend you most want to be around and the friend who makes you laugh and smile. God also wants to be the friend you talk to when you're sad, lonely, or hurting. He's the friend who is always there for you.

This journal gives you lots of fun and creative ways to spend time with God. As you spend more time with Him, you'll get to know Him so much better. Think about what happens when you hang out with your best friend. When you spend a lot of time with someone, you start acting like that person. You may talk the way she does or do things the way she does. You aren't even trying to do this—it just happens. And that's what happens when you spend time with God.

I've included lots of things to think and pray about in this journal. I've also included lots of short Scripture verses and prayers. There's space after each of these for you to write your own prayer or whatever God puts on your mind. You can journal anything! You could even write a poem or a story. It's totally up to you!

The more time you spend with God, the more you become like Him. You'll also find that the more you pray, the easier it gets. In fact, it's as easy as talking to your best friend!

Prayer might seem confusing and intimidating and complicated, but it's not. Prayer is simply having a conversation with God. It's talking to Him like you would a friend. You don't have to use big words or think of fancy things to say. You can talk to God respectfully, kindly, and pretty much like you talk to your friends. But you can also be honest with Him about how you are feeling, including your doubts, worries, and fears. Right now, without even thinking too much about it, write a quick note to God. Pretend you're sending a text to your best friend.

Meet Four of God's Girls

These are four sisters who love Jesus and share their likes, thoughts, and ideas with you throughout this book!

Alena, age 16, played the character Danielle Jordan in the movie *War Room*. Besides acting, she's also written fiction books for girls and loves to sing. Like all of her sisters, she's super grounded in her faith and loves sharing about Jesus.

Kaitlyn, age 14, is an extrovert who enjoys gymnastics and baking and is up for just about anything. She adores conversation and hanging out with people.

Camryn, age 11, is the "older" twin. She's an art lover who also participates in dance and soccer. Full of determination, she always gives her all to everything she does.

Olivia, age 11, is the "younger" twin. Creativity is totally her thing—she's all about acting, writing, painting, and singing. She's even done some photography and videography.

> **"Rejoice always, pray continually, give thanks in all circumstances; for this is God's will for you in Christ Jesus"** (1 Thessalonians 5:16-18).

God loves it when you talk to Him. And remember that praying is not only you talking to God—He loves to talk to you too! Be sure to leave quiet space in your conversations so He can speak to your heart. Maybe even turn on some quiet worship music. It can help you sit in the quiet and open your heart.

What are some times in your day when you can pray? (Remember that you can pray out loud as well as quietly to yourself.)

_____

_____

_____

_____

_____

_____

_____

_____

_____

Dear God,

Thank You so much for loving me! Thank You for always being there for me to talk to. Sometimes it feels weird because I can't see You, but help me to remember that You are with me all the time. Teach me how to pray and how to listen so that I can know You better.

In Jesus' name, amen.

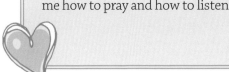

Praying is a lot more than just asking God to help you. Prayer is how we build a relationship with God. It's the same way we get to know a friend better. God wants us to talk to Him, and He wants to talk to us.

Things I want to tell God...

_____
_____
_____
_____
_____
_____
_____

Things God is telling me...

_____
_____
_____
_____
_____
_____
_____

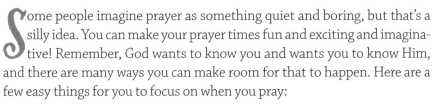

Some people imagine prayer as something quiet and boring, but that's a silly idea. You can make your prayer times fun and exciting and imaginative! Remember, God wants to know you and wants you to know Him, and there are many ways you can make room for that to happen. Here are a few easy things for you to focus on when you pray:

Praise. Worship God! You get to pick how. Sing a song to Him. Dance for Him. Draw or paint a picture for Him. You can express how you feel about God in lots of ways, so go ahead and be creative!

Thanks. There is so much to be thankful for today! What can you think of? Choose one or two things and write them down. You can always go back in your memory to remind yourself what God has done for you.

Others. Pray for other people—your mom, dad, brothers, sisters, friends, teachers, neighbors...If God brings anyone to your mind, talk about them with God and ask Him to meet their needs.

You. What do you need help with? Write it all down and talk to God about the needs in your own life. Remember, He cares!

Confession. What are some sins you need to ask God to forgive you for? Talking to God about the areas where you didn't follow God's way will always remind you of how much you need Him. You can always count on God to forgive you. Find 1 John 1:9 in your Bible and write it out on the next page.

1 John 1:9

_____
_____
_____
_____
_____
_____

My prayer for today...

_____
_____
_____
_____
_____
_____
_____
_____

> **"Devote yourselves to prayer, being watchful and thankful"**
> (Colossians 4:2).

God wants you to talk to Him about everything—anytime you want. You can talk to Him about your homework, your favorite foods, a fight you had with a friend, or even the weather! What are your favorite things to talk about with God?

_____

_____

_____

_____

_____

_____

_____

_____

I like to talk with God about everything! I talk to Him all through the day. I'm a "slow processor." Talking to Him helps me to process through the things going on in my life. — **Alena**

Dear God,

I'm so glad I can talk to You whenever I want! Help me to remember how important it is to pray so I can have a better friendship with You for my whole life!

In Jesus' name, amen.

_____

_____

_____

_____

_____

_____

_____

_____

_____

_____

_____

_____

What things have happened in your life that you will never, ever forget? Meeting your best friend, winning a talent show, becoming a big sister. Has God helped you in a difficult time when no one else could help? Whatever you remember, these things probably changed your life forever, and that's the reason they matter a lot.

Make a list of things that God has done in your life. Whenever you start to have doubts that God is giving you good things, read your list. It won't take you long to remember that God will do crazy things in your life when you trust in Him!

_____

_____

_____

_____

_____

_____

_____

_____

_____

_____

_____

_____

_____

_____

Dear God,

Thank You for every good thing in my life You have given me. And help me to recognize what You have done when I miss it! When I stop and think about it, there is so much! Help me to be grateful and confident that You have given me everything I need in order to do what You want me to do.

In Jesus' name, amen.

What are you grateful for today? Write a letter thanking God for the things
He has given you.

_____

_____

_____

_____

_____

_____

_____

_____

_____

_____

_____

_____

_____

_____

_____

_____

_____

_____

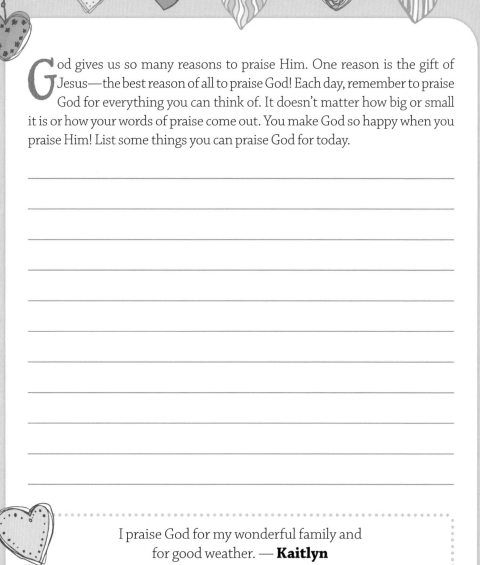

God gives us so many reasons to praise Him. One reason is the gift of Jesus—the best reason of all to praise God! Each day, remember to praise God for everything you can think of. It doesn't matter how big or small it is or how your words of praise come out. You make God so happy when you praise Him! List some things you can praise God for today.

_____

_____

_____

_____

_____

_____

_____

_____

_____

_____

_____

I praise God for my wonderful family and
for good weather. — **Kaitlyn**

I praise God that we have
food, water, and shelter. — **Olivia**

Do you ever wonder about God's plans for you? What are some things He might have planned for you this year? What are some of your dreams for this year?

_____

_____

_____

_____

_____

_____

_____

_____

_____

_____

_____

_____

_____

_____

Dear God,

Thank You for giving my life a purpose! I know You have so many special things for me to do. Help me to never be so comfortable doing what feels good to me that I don't want to do what You need me to do. Inspire me and lead me toward Your plan.

In Jesus' name, amen.

Write a letter to yourself! Describe what you want to happen in the next year, what you want to do, what you are expecting to happen, and what are the main prayers in your heart. After you write it, don't look at it for a month, six months, or a year. When it is time, look back at this letter and compare what you wrote to how that time actually went. Dream big—and always trust that God will surprise you!

Dear God,

Thank You for giving me such a great imagination to think and dream about what my future could look like. Please give me wisdom as I walk toward the plans You have for me. Most of all, direct my steps. I know You are writing a beautiful story with my life as I continue to follow You.

In Jesus' name, amen.

Are you the kind of person who likes to make decisions? Or are you someone who would rather let someone else decide? Either way, every day you face a lot of choices. In fact, research says that you face about 3,000 decisions a day. You choose to obey or disobey your parents. You choose to do your homework or waste time. You choose to walk or run. You choose to gossip or speak nicely about people. You choose to react in anger or in love. In every decision, God knows what the *best* decision is. And when you stay connected to Him in prayer, you can make the best decision too!

Write down the decisions you make today. See how long your list gets before you run out of space! Then go back and try to figure out if you made the *best* decision.

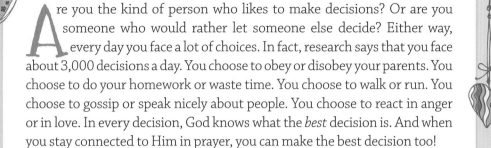

_____

_____

_____

_____

_____

_____

_____

_____

_____

_____

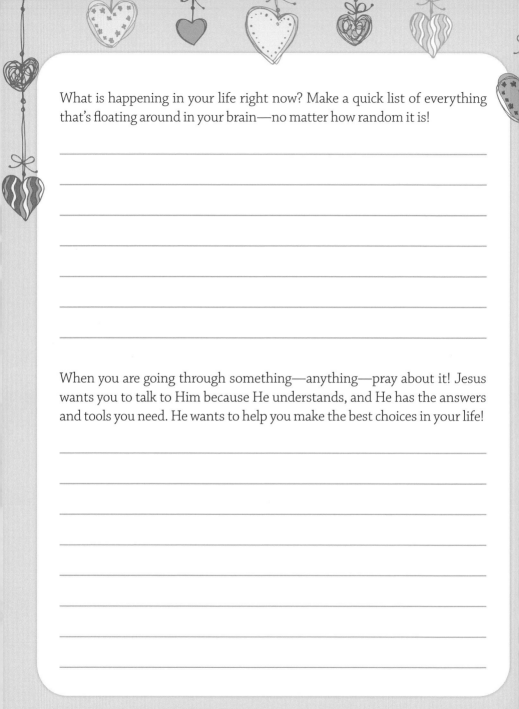

What is happening in your life right now? Make a quick list of everything that's floating around in your brain—no matter how random it is!

_____

_____

_____

_____

_____

_____

When you are going through something—anything—pray about it! Jesus wants you to talk to Him because He understands, and He has the answers and tools you need. He wants to help you make the best choices in your life!

_____

_____

_____

_____

_____

_____

_____

_____

Dear God,

Thank You for loving me so much that You want me to be wise and make wise choices. I know wisdom comes only from You! Help me to trust that You will help me make the *best* decisions, both now and later. And help me to focus on what You want me to do as I live for You today.

In Jesus' name, amen.

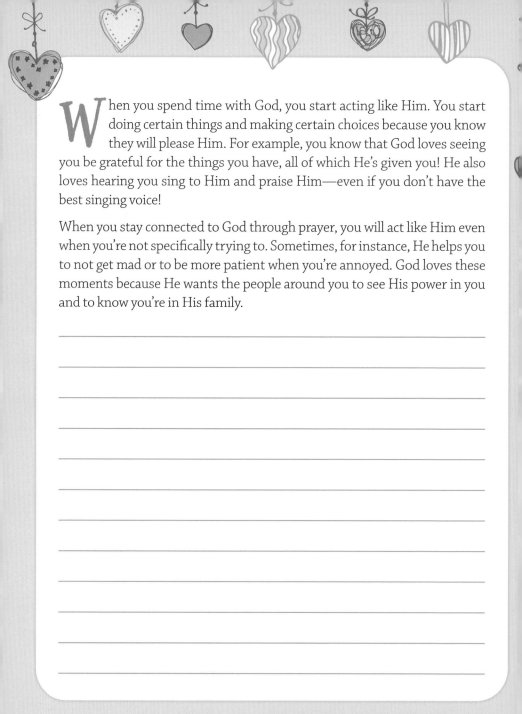

When you spend time with God, you start acting like Him. You start doing certain things and making certain choices because you know they will please Him. For example, you know that God loves seeing you be grateful for the things you have, all of which He's given you! He also loves hearing you sing to Him and praise Him—even if you don't have the best singing voice!

When you stay connected to God through prayer, you will act like Him even when you're not specifically trying to. Sometimes, for instance, He helps you to not get mad or to be more patient when you're annoyed. God loves these moments because He wants the people around you to see His power in you and to know you're in His family.

Your relationship with God should be the most important thing in your life! If you ever find yourself stuck about what to pray for, pray that you are always putting Him first in your life. What are some ways you can put God first?

_____

_____

_____

_____

_____

_____

_____

_____

_____

_____

_____

I like to read my Bible right when I get up, before turning on the TV or doing anything else. — **Kaitlyn**

I put Him first by thanking Him for a great day. — **Camryn**

Dear God,

Thank You for allowing me to have such a close relationship with You. Please help me to always put You first in my life. Help me to remember that You are loving, You are smart, You are patient, and You are creative. Help me to stay connected to You at all times, and please help me grow in my understanding of how much You love me.

In Jesus' name, amen.

K eeping a journal is a great way to remember all the seasons in your life. It may seem impossible now, but I promise, one day you will start to forget some of the details. Writing about your life in a journal like this is a great way to always remember what God has done for you.

What do you want to remember about your life right now?

_____

_____

_____

_____

_____

_____

_____

_____

_____

_____

_____

_____

_____

_____

_____

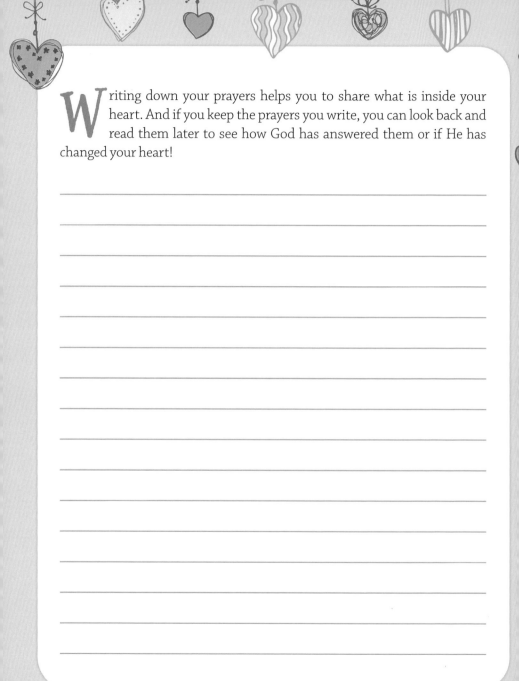

Writing down your prayers helps you to share what is inside your heart. And if you keep the prayers you write, you can look back and read them later to see how God has answered them or if He has changed your heart!

Dear God,

Sometimes when I have a dream that doesn't come true, it's really easy for me to feel like I failed or did something wrong—especially when everyone around me seems to be doing amazing things. Everyone but me. Help me to keep dreaming big because I know that You want to do incredible things in my life.

In Jesus' name, amen.

_____

_____

_____

_____

_____

_____

_____

_____

_____

_____

_____

We often try to change our hearts by making sure we do the right thing, but that's not the way it works. God wants more from us than actions that look good; He wants us to *be* good on the inside. He wants His Holy Spirit inside us to bring out that good. He wants to change our hearts so that we are honest, sincere, genuine, loving, and all the good things that make us more like Jesus.

The Bible says we can know if someone is God's child by the way she lives her life. When you become more and more like God, His love grows in your heart and changes you from the inside out. His Spirit changes the way you think, the way you act, and even the way you feel. God wants His presence inside us to grow so that others will see Him when they look at us.

God wants you to be strong and beautiful on the inside and on the outside. Write a prayer asking for God to change you from the inside out.

_____

_____

_____

_____

_____

_____

_____

_____

_____

_____

_____

_____

Make a list of ways you can be beautiful on the inside and on the outside. When you're finished with your list, circle which of these ways are most pleasing to God.

_____

_____

_____

_____

_____

_____

_____

_____

_____

_____

_____

_____

_____

_____

_____

_____

_____

_____

> "The fruit that the Spirit produces in a person's life is love, joy, peace, patience, kindness, goodness, faithfulness, gentleness, and self-control"
> (Galatians 5:22-23 ERV).

God has planted His Spirit in your heart like a seed in the ground. And that seed grows what the Bible calls the fruit of the Spirit—love, joy, peace, patience, kindness, goodness, faithfulness, gentleness, and self-control. They grow in your life when you walk closely with God, read His Word, and talk to Him throughout the day. Write down what you think each part of the fruit of the Spirit could look like in your life.

Love: _____

Joy: _____

Peace: _____

Patience: _____

Kindness: _____

Goodness: _____

Faithfulness: _____

Gentleness: _____

Self-control: _____

Dear God,

Thank You for growing the fruit of Your Spirit inside me. I know I don't always act or speak the way You would act or speak. I am so glad You love me and want to help me be more like You. Please fill me with Your love, joy, peace, patience, kindness, goodness, faithfulness, gentleness, and self-control. I want my actions and words to give people a taste of You.

In Jesus' name, amen.

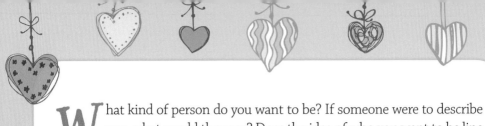

W hat kind of person do you want to be? If someone were to describe you, what would they say? Does the idea of who you want to be line up with who you are now? If not, how can you ask God to change this?

_____

_____

_____

_____

_____

_____

_____

_____

_____

_____

_____

_____

God is helping me to become kind in an intentional way. If you make an effort to see people through God's eyes, then you can really "see" them and how beautiful they really are. — **Alena**

When you are feeling sad because of something, you can talk to God instead of worrying. You can always throw your cares and worries to God because He cares deeply about you and loves to help you in any and every situation. Use this space to write down the situations that are making you worry, and then talk to God about them. He promises to help you—always!

_____

_____

_____

_____

_____

_____

_____

_____

_____

_____

_____

_____

_____

_____

_____

Dear God,

I feel happy when things in my life are going great, and I feel sad when things in my life aren't going well. Thank You for making it possible for me to have joy in *any* situation because You love me, You forgive me, and You promise to take care of me. Help me not to worry, but to trust You always.

In Jesus' name, amen.

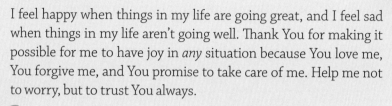

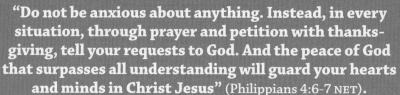

"Do not be anxious about anything. Instead, in every situation, through prayer and petition with thanksgiving, tell your requests to God. And the peace of God that surpasses all understanding will guard your hearts and minds in Christ Jesus" (Philippians 4:6-7 NET).

_____
_____
_____
_____
_____
_____
_____
_____
_____
_____
_____
_____
_____
_____
_____
_____

Fear can keep you from trying new things, and it can also stop you from doing everything God has planned for you to do. That is not what God wants, and I'm pretty sure that is not what you want either! Your feelings may say that you should be afraid, but God says different! If you fill your mind with God's truth, it becomes easier to trust Him even when you feel afraid. Write down everything you're afraid of—from spiders to feeling lonely to earthquakes. Feeling fear is normal, but God can help you live with courage too.

_____

_____

_____

_____

_____

_____

_____

_____

_____

_____

_____

Now look at your list and pray specifically about everything on it. Tell God how you feel, and ask Him to cover your fear with His power and His love!

Even if you're a super-adventurous girl, it can be a challenge to try new things or to make yourself do hard things! Write down some things you'd love to try—riding a zip line, learning a new instrument, making a new friend, figuring out how to build a campfire, baking a loaf of bread…It could be anything! Then ask God to give you the courage to start trying new things today!

_____

_____

_____

_____

_____

_____

_____

_____

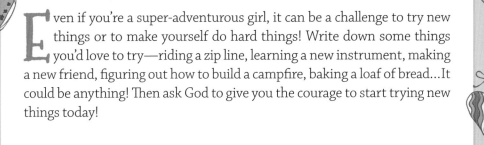

Someday I would like to try skydiving! Or something extreme, like climbing Mount Everest or something! — **Alena**

Hmmm. Skydiving sounds cool. I'd also like to try going on a cruise someday. — **Kaitlyn**

I would like to go *scuba* diving. — **Camryn**

Scuba diving! Yes! Me too! — **Olivia**

Dear God,

Thank You for giving me Your peace. I am so grateful that I am Your daughter and that Your peace lives inside me. Sometimes I forget that I don't need to worry about things, or I try to fix my problems on my own. Please help me to trust You more. I thank You for always helping me to say no to worry and yes to peace.

In Jesus' name, amen.

It's not always easy to love people—especially when those people are mean to you or just aren't very nice to anyone. But if we're saying yes to God and following Him, we can learn how to love people even when we don't want to or don't feel like it. When you begin to understand God's amazing love, you can rely on His power to help you love even those people who are hard to love.

_____

_____

_____

_____

_____

_____

_____

_____

_____

_____

I feel protective of people. So I love people when others are mean by standing up for them. Mean people can make me angry. But God has taught me to love even the people who are mean to others. They are His children too. — **Camryn**

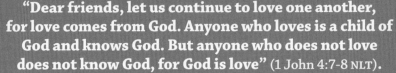

"Dear friends, let us continue to love one another, for love comes from God. Anyone who loves is a child of God and knows God. But anyone who does not love does not know God, for God is love" (1 John 4:7-8 NLT).

Jesus loved the people around Him in so many different ways:

- *He served those in need.* "Do as I did: The Son of Man did not come for people to serve him. He came to serve others and to give his life to save many people" (Matthew 20:28 ERV).

- *He said only what God told Him to say.* "What I taught was not from myself. The Father who sent me told me what to say and what to teach" (John 12:49 ERV).

- *He showed God's love to everyone.* "Come to me, all you who are weary and burdened, and I will give you rest" (Matthew 11:28).

_____

_____

_____

_____

_____

_____

_____

_____

_____

_____

_____

_____

_____

> **"Treat others in the same way
> that you would want them to treat you"**
> (Luke 6:31 NET).

Kindness may be contagious (that means you can catch it!), but being kind isn't always easy. Being kind requires that we think of those around us instead of thinking only about ourselves, and that way of living definitely requires help from God. Write a prayer asking God to help you learn how to show kindness to others, or make a list of ways you can be kind to the people around you. Ask Him for His power to live it out!

_____

_____

_____

_____

_____

_____

_____

_____

_____

_____

_____

Dear God,

Thank You for Jesus' example of gentleness. When I hurt, please help me not to lash out in anger. Help me to be gentle with my words and actions when it would be easier to be harsh. Help me to be calm and kind. Please continue to grow Your gentleness in me.

In Jesus' name, amen.

Read Matthew 22:39 and Luke 6:31. Make a list of what makes you feel loved. Maybe it is when someone writes you a nice note or saves you a seat.

_____

_____

_____

_____

_____

_____

_____

_____

_____

_____

_____

_____

_____

_____

_____

_____

Now look at your list and choose a few of those things to do for someone else!

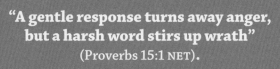

"A gentle response turns away anger,
but a harsh word stirs up wrath"
(Proverbs 15:1 NET).

"You are the light of the world.
A town built on a hill cannot be hidden"
(Matthew 5:14).

Dear God,

Thank You for trusting me with words. I know You did not have to give me so many words to express how I am feeling, but I am thankful You did. Sometimes it is hard to speak kindly, but I pray You will help me! Help me to use my words to show others Your love.

In Jesus' name, amen.

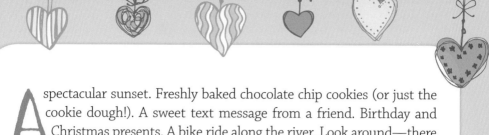

A spectacular sunset. Freshly baked chocolate chip cookies (or just the cookie dough!). A sweet text message from a friend. Birthday and Christmas presents. A bike ride along the river. Look around—there are so many things in life that show God's love for you! Take a few minutes to write down all the things in your life that remind you of God's love.

_____

_____

_____

_____

_____

_____

_____

_____

_____

_____

_____

_____

_____

_____

_____

_____

_____

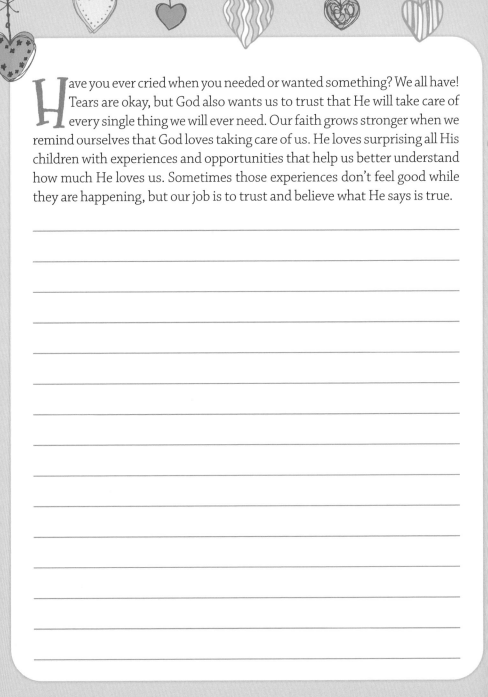

Have you ever cried when you needed or wanted something? We all have! Tears are okay, but God also wants us to trust that He will take care of every single thing we will ever need. Our faith grows stronger when we remind ourselves that God loves taking care of us. He loves surprising all His children with experiences and opportunities that help us better understand how much He loves us. Sometimes those experiences don't feel good while they are happening, but our job is to trust and believe what He says is true.

Dear God,

I am so glad I can trust You. I know that You have a wonderful adventure planned for my life, and I want to enjoy all of it. Help me to do the things You ask me to do even when I don't understand everything or know how things are going to turn out. Help me to have faith in You and to be faithful to You.

In Jesus' name, amen.

_____

_____

_____

_____

_____

What do you need to trust God to take care of today? Tomorrow? Next week? Next year? Write them down and then look back later to see how God helped you!

_____

_____

_____

_____

_____

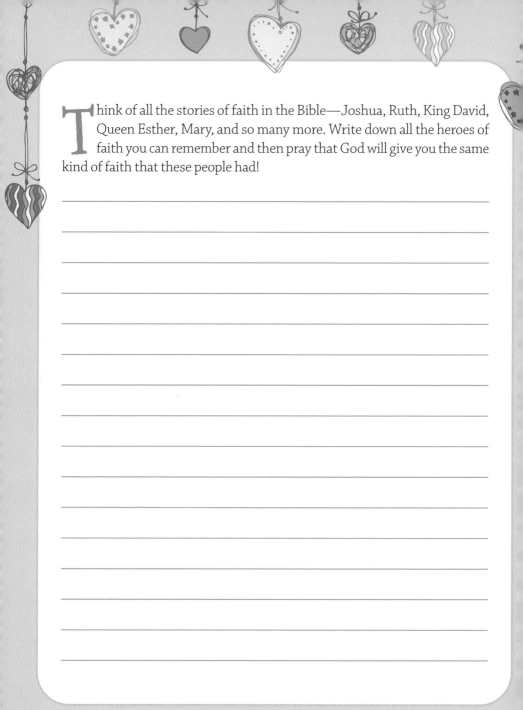

Think of all the stories of faith in the Bible—Joshua, Ruth, King David, Queen Esther, Mary, and so many more. Write down all the heroes of faith you can remember and then pray that God will give you the same kind of faith that these people had!

Dear God,

Thank You for all the stories of faith in the Bible. I want to have crazy faith too! Will You help me not to be afraid to ask You for what seems impossible? Help me to trust that You will do what is best for my life even when I do not understand it.

In Jesus' name, amen.

If you struggle with being patient, you are not alone. I am actually not a fan of long things—long lines, long days, long books, long walks...Get the idea? I like things to happen as quickly as possible. So I would say that being patient is definitely something I have to ask for help with all the time—and I am so glad God is always willing to help me, no matter how many times I ask. He has also taught me that some things take time, and it's best to wait for them.

_____

_____

_____

_____

_____

_____

_____

_____

_____

_____

_____

_____

_____

When you're waiting for something, the best way to make the time pass more quickly is to do something else! Write down a list of things you can do—read a book, sort through your clothes, make a smoothie, play a game, paint your nails…There are lots of things you can do while you wait.

_____

_____

_____

_____

_____

_____

_____

_____

_____

_____

I'm not the best at waiting. But I like to do hair. I'll do my sisters' hair or practice on some dolls. — **Camryn**

I like painting, doing art. — **Olivia**

Dear God,

I pray that You will help me grow in patience. Sometimes I get impatient and would rather have what I want instead of waiting for what You or my parents or other people have for me. Please help me to be patient with life the way You are patient with me. I don't want to miss the great things you have for me now or in the future. I'm so grateful You are always patient with me!

In Jesus' name, amen.

Instead of worrying about how to make sure everyone likes you, use your energy to make sure everyone sees Jesus in you. Here are two ways the Bible says you can do that:

- Luke 6:31 says, "Do to others as you would have them do to you."
- Matthew 22:39 says, "Love your neighbor as yourself."

How can you let others see Jesus in you today?

_____

_____

_____

_____

_____

_____

_____

_____

_____

_____

_____

_____

_____

Did you know that your relationship with God is not just about you? God wants you to share His message of love and grace with other people too! You can share His message by telling other people about Jesus, serving others, and teaching people things you have learned about God. When you're talking to God, make sure that besides talking to Him about your own stuff, you are also talking to Him about others!

_____

_____

_____

_____

_____

_____

_____

_____

_____

When I pray for others I usually pray
for their health and safety. — **Kaitlyn**

I pray that others have a good day. — **Camryn**

I ask God to make them stronger in faith. — **Olivia**

Dear God,

Thank You for giving me a relationship with You through Jesus. Help me to always practice sharing Your love and the message of Jesus with others so they will know You too. Thank You for loving me, and please help me to love everyone because You do!

In Jesus' name, amen.

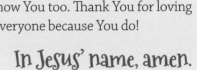

"Think about what is good and worthy of praise.
Think about what is true and honorable and right and
pure and beautiful and respected" (Philippians 4:8 ERV).

Always be willing to praise God, no matter what is happening in your life. Sometimes things will happen that make you feel as if God is far away, but don't ever believe that. God is always close by, and He is always ready to listen. If you're not sure exactly *how* to praise God, you can start by reading some of your favorite Bible verses (I recommend Psalms) or singing some of your favorite worship songs. Or just thank God for His love and care!

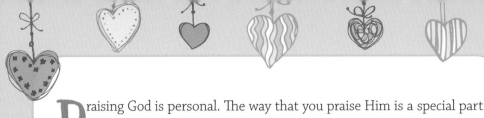

Praising God is personal. The way that you praise Him is a special part of your relationship with Him! How do you praise God? Do you have something to praise Him for today?

_____

_____

_____

_____

_____

_____

_____

_____

_____

_____

_____

_____

I praise God with singing and through being
kind to others. — **Kaitlyn**

Dear God,

You are so good to me! I am grateful that You want to fill me with Your goodness. Please help me focus on You regardless of what is happening around me. Teach me to "think about what is good and worthy of praise...what is true and honorable and right and pure and beautiful and respected" (Philippians 4:8 ERV) so that my words, actions, and attitudes can better reflect Your goodness.

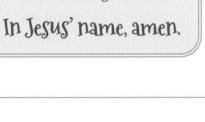

In Jesus' name, amen.

For our own good, God wants us to have self-control. This means knowing when we have had enough of something and when we need to stop. Think about when you might need to say no to...

- speaking words that might upset a friend
- thinking thoughts that don't make you feel good
- participating in activities that might sound fun but could be harmful
- spending time on social media and other screens

You can pray and ask God to help you say no to the things that aren't helping you.

There are some things in life that you can control (like getting up when your alarm goes off, choosing friends who help you grow, and getting your homework done right away), and there are other things you can't control (like the pages and pages of math problems your teacher assigned, chores you're responsible for, or getting sick before a big dance performance or basketball game). When you find yourself in a situation you can't control, ask God for His help. And also ask Him to help you with the things you *can* control.

Things I can control today...

_____

_____

_____

Things I can't control today...

_____

_____

_____

My prayer for today...

_____

_____

_____

Dear God,

Thank You for reminding me that life is best lived when it's under control. Under *Your* control. And thank You that when I give You control, You are not selfish with me. You provide everything I need, and I never have to worry. Thank You for growing me up and teaching me to live with self-control. Please help me to live my life in a way that helps others see how good life with You can be.

In Jesus' name, amen.

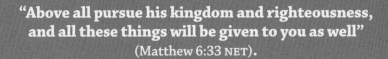

"Above all pursue his kingdom and righteousness,
and all these things will be given to you as well"
(Matthew 6:33 NET).

> **"Do not conform to the pattern of this world, but be transformed by the renewing of your mind"**
> (Romans 12:2).

The Bible tells us that we should not try to fit in or be like someone else. We should only want to be like Jesus and do and have what He says is good for us! When you try to be like Jesus, you don't have to worry about fitting in. You can just be you! Can you think of a time that you wanted to fit in?

_____

_____

_____

_____

_____

What can you do today to try to be more like Christ?

_____

_____

_____

_____

_____

_____

**"Direct my footsteps
according to your word"**
(Psalm 119:133).

Pray and ask God to help you to have a goal for your life, and make sure you ask Him to guide you in what you do!

_____

_____

_____

_____

_____

_____

_____

_____

_____

_____

_____

_____

_____

Are you more of a leader or a follower? Or does it depend on the situation? God actually tells us that leaders need to be followers! Serving others—and putting their needs before our own—is the best way to lead. No matter how you see yourself, you can both lead others and follow God. He will show you how!

_____

_____

_____

_____

_____

_____

_____

I become a leader when everyone else is falling apart. Difficult times force me to get my head in the game. I lead best by following God, by praying to Him, and by seeking Him out in the situation. And humbling myself. — **Alena**

I can lead just by helping others. Especially through tough times. And reading the Bible, of course. — **Camryn**

When I help others I am leading them *and* following God at the same time. I also follow Him by worshipping Him and praying to Him. — **Olivia**

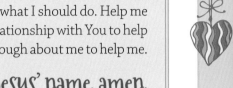

Dear God,

I know You have given me everything I need! No matter what situation I am in, Your Word will guide me in what I should do. Help me to use what I know about You and my relationship with You to help me grow. I'm so grateful that You care enough about me to help me.

In Jesus' name, amen.

Sometimes it's hard to speak up and ask questions—like in class when you don't understand something. You don't want to sound clueless or draw attention to yourself. But asking questions is one of the best ways to learn! And often, someone else (or everyone else!) is also confused and wondering the same thing you're wondering.

God wants you to ask Him all the questions you have—all the time! Ask Him questions about Himself. About your life. About what He is doing. About anything at all. He hears you, and He promises to answer you.

Things I wonder about...

_____

_____

_____

_____

_____

_____

_____

_____

_____

_____

_____

Sometimes I wonder if God exists. — **Alena**

Sometimes I wonder if He is listening. — **Kaitlyn**

Sometimes I wonder what heaven is like. — **Camryn**

Sometimes I wonder what it will be like to live
in heaven forever. Eternity is a long time! — **Olivia**

Dear God,

Thank You that I know Your name and can call on You when I need You or when I just feel like talking. Thank You for being my support and strength. Help me to stay connected to You, and remind me to seek You when I feel discouraged or far away, because You always know just what I need.

In Jesus' name, amen.

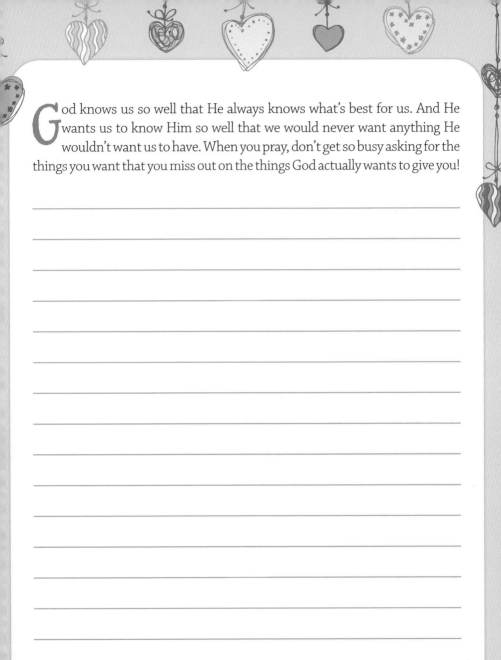

God knows us so well that He always knows what's best for us. And He wants us to know Him so well that we would never want anything He wouldn't want us to have. When you pray, don't get so busy asking for the things you want that you miss out on the things God actually wants to give you!

What are some things I want right now?

_____
_____
_____
_____
_____
_____
_____

What are some things God wants for me?

_____
_____
_____
_____
_____
_____
_____
_____

Dear God,

It makes me so happy to know I can ask You for anything! I want what You know is best for me. Will You help me to spend time getting to know You better? I know You want only what is best for my life, and I am grateful that You take care of me.

In Jesus' name, amen.

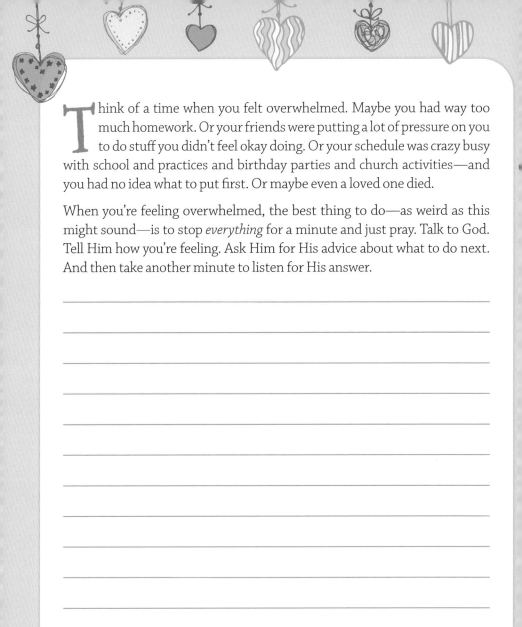

Think of a time when you felt overwhelmed. Maybe you had way too much homework. Or your friends were putting a lot of pressure on you to do stuff you didn't feel okay doing. Or your schedule was crazy busy with school and practices and birthday parties and church activities—and you had no idea what to put first. Or maybe even a loved one died.

When you're feeling overwhelmed, the best thing to do—as weird as this might sound—is to stop *everything* for a minute and just pray. Talk to God. Tell Him how you're feeling. Ask Him for His advice about what to do next. And then take another minute to listen for His answer.

Has God ever helped you do something you were really afraid to do? Maybe you did it and it was great, or maybe it wasn't great but God helped you through it anyway. Describe what happened and how God showed you that you can really do all things with His strength!

_____

_____

_____

_____

_____

_____

_____

_____

_____

_____

_____

_____

I used to be really scared to flip and do back handstands in gymnastics. But over time God has given me the confidence to do them. —**Kaitlyn**

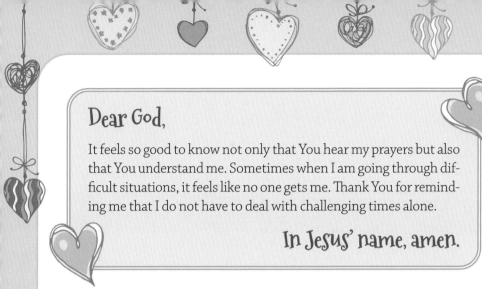

Dear God,

It feels so good to know not only that You hear my prayers but also that You understand me. Sometimes when I am going through difficult situations, it feels like no one gets me. Thank You for reminding me that I do not have to deal with challenging times alone.

In Jesus' name, amen.

> **"The LORD is close to the brokenhearted and saves those who are crushed in spirit"**
> (Psalm 34:18).

God's love is still there even when bad things happen. He has not forgotten you. He understands your difficult feelings, and He wants you to know that He cares about everything you go through. God wants you to come to Him for comfort even if you don't understand what He is doing. The Bible says that God's plans always work out!

_____

_____

_____

_____

_____

_____

_____

_____

_____

_____

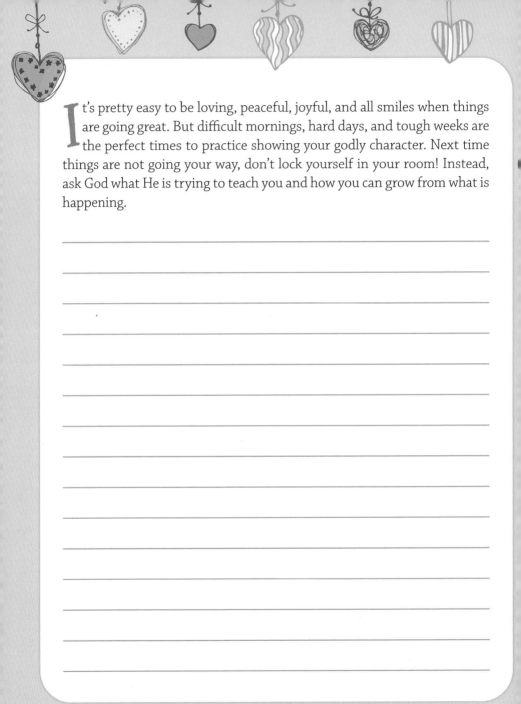

It's pretty easy to be loving, peaceful, joyful, and all smiles when things are going great. But difficult mornings, hard days, and tough weeks are the perfect times to practice showing your godly character. Next time things are not going your way, don't lock yourself in your room! Instead, ask God what He is trying to teach you and how you can grow from what is happening.

Things that make God happy:

_____

_____

_____

_____

_____

Things that make God sad:

_____

_____

_____

_____

_____

Ways I want to change my thoughts and actions:

_____

_____

_____

_____

_____

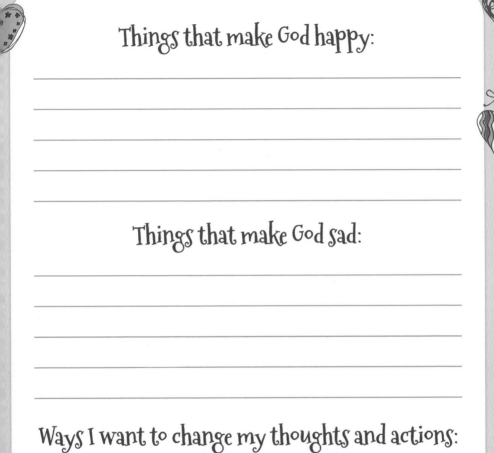

Friends are awesome, but have you ever found yourself wanting to be like them or wishing you had the things they had? When you do this too much, you can get jealous of them—and that's not good. When you notice this happening, ask God to help you focus on the things you admire about your friends while thanking Him that He made you just the way you are!

Things I admire about my friends...

_____

_____

_____

_____

_____

_____

Things I love about the way God made me...

_____

_____

_____

_____

_____

_____

Dear God,

Thank You for giving me friends who are so special. I am grateful that You made each of us so different. Sometimes it is hard not to want to be like others because I think they are so great! Will You help me to realize how special I am too? Help me to know that just because I am different does not make me less valuable than anyone else.

In Jesus' name, amen.

God does not just see the things you are doing. Nope! He also sees you on the inside and knows your heart. He sees what you feel. He knows what you worry about, what makes your heart happy, and what you are afraid of. God knows exactly what you are going through even if you have never told anyone else. He knows when you want to do the right things but you just don't know how, and He even knows when you don't really want to do the right thing at all!

Take a moment to write down your thoughts about God seeing you on the outside as well as the inside, and ask Him to help you always do the right thing.

_____

_____

_____

_____

_____

_____

_____

_____

_____

Guess what? You just wrote a really amazing prayer! I'm so proud of you—and God is too!

Did you know that the way to tell what a girl is really like is by what she does when nobody is watching?

How do you treat others when a parent or teacher isn't watching? How well do you clean a room of your house when nobody is watching (and when nobody is going to check to see how well you cleaned)? How hard would you work on a school assignment if you knew your teacher wasn't going to grade it?

God doesn't expect you to be perfect, but He loves to see you do your best. So remember that even when nobody seems to care what you do, God cares!

_____

_____

_____

_____

_____

_____

_____

_____

_____

_____

_____

Dear God,

Thank You for seeing me and knowing me. Will You help me to love You and to show Your love to others, even when it feels like no one is watching? I am happy to know that I am not alone! Help me to feel safe and know You are there for me, even when I don't see You.

In Jesus' name, amen.

Have you ever gone off on a friend or sibling when they've done something bad or silly? It's hard not to, but the better thing to do is to pray for them instead. You can ask God to place His Spirit in them. God wants to change more than their behavior today; He wants to change their lives forever! Loving people when you disagree with what they're saying or doing means praying for them. When you want to change someone else, remember to ask God to change you.

- Read James 4:8 and pray, "Lord, help us to draw close to You."
- Read Romans 12:10 and pray, "Lord, help me to love them and to look for ways to show them Your love."

The best way to show love for someone is to pray for him or her! If someone is making you sad or you're worried about them, say this prayer for them:

Dear God,

I know You see the problems I am having with _____. I know You love them, and I pray that You will show them Your love. I know I need to love them too. Will You fill _____'s heart with joy? Help _____ with anything hard that they are dealing with, and help me to be patient and kind to them.

In Jesus' name, amen.

God loves it when you pray for your friends! Write down a list of friends to pray for and what to pray for them. It's always fun to look back and see how God answered your prayers!

We all have special gifts and talents and things we enjoy doing. Even if we aren't 100 percent sure of our gifts and talents, God is! So don't stress if you don't know exactly what they are right now. Just pray and ask God to help you figure it out! And while you are waiting, don't be afraid to try new things.

Use this space to brainstorm how you can use your talents. Remember that whatever your gifts are, God can use them to bless others. For example, you could use your talents to make crafts as gifts for friends, write a song for your baby sister, or color or draw a picture for your teacher.

I can use my talents for speaking or singing. They both give the words to others that they sometimes feel that they cannot form for themselves. —**Alena**

One of my talents is writing. I can bless others with my writing because it helps them to read about other people who are going through the same things that they are. —**Camryn**

Dear God,

Thank You for making me, and thank You for giving me gifts and talents! Help me to remember that You purposely made me different from other people. My skills, gifts, and talents are all very special and unique. Please show me how I can use them to bless other people. Help me not to be shy or embarrassed but to be confident because You have given them to me.

In Jesus' name, amen.

"Bear with each other and forgive one another if any of you has a grievance against someone. Forgive as the Lord forgave you" (Colossians 3:13).

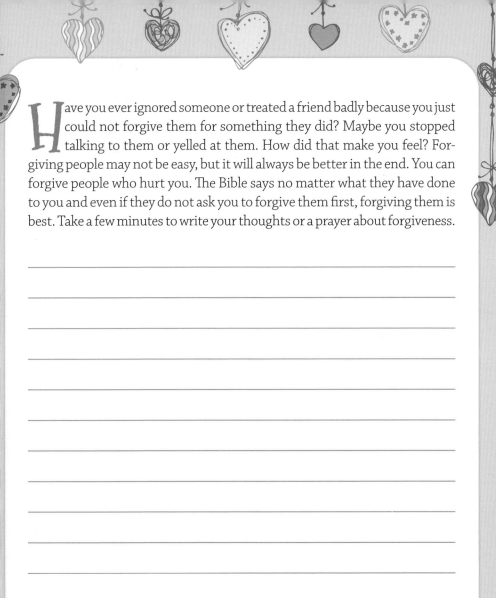

Have you ever ignored someone or treated a friend badly because you just could not forgive them for something they did? Maybe you stopped talking to them or yelled at them. How did that make you feel? Forgiving people may not be easy, but it will always be better in the end. You can forgive people who hurt you. The Bible says no matter what they have done to you and even if they do not ask you to forgive them first, forgiving them is best. Take a few minutes to write your thoughts or a prayer about forgiveness.

_____

_____

_____

_____

_____

_____

_____

_____

_____

_____

_____

_____

_____

_____

_____

When someone does something mean to you or something you think is unfair, the best thing to do is to talk to God about it. It really helps to write it down and then pray for that person. You can also write down the things you have done that you need to ask God to forgive.

Dear God,

I am grateful that You do not let the things I do wrong push me away from You. Instead, You forgive me and bring me closer to You. Help me to believe that I am forgiven regardless of how bad a mistake I make. Also, please help me to forgive others when they hurt me. Thank You so much for Your gift of forgiveness!

In Jesus' name, amen.

Are you super busy with stuff—homework, sports or music practice, time with friends and family, church activities, chores and responsibilities? Most of us have schedules that are so packed, we forget to take time to rest and spend time with God. But time with God should be the most important part of your day! Write down your daily or weekly schedule, and then write in times to rest and spend time talking to God.

_____

_____

_____

_____

_____

_____

_____

_____

_____

_____

_____

_____

_____

_____

_____

Dear God,

Thank You for helping me to know when I need to rest and take the time to pray and talk to You. I want to be awake and alert so I can hear and see everything You have for me!

In Jesus' name, amen.

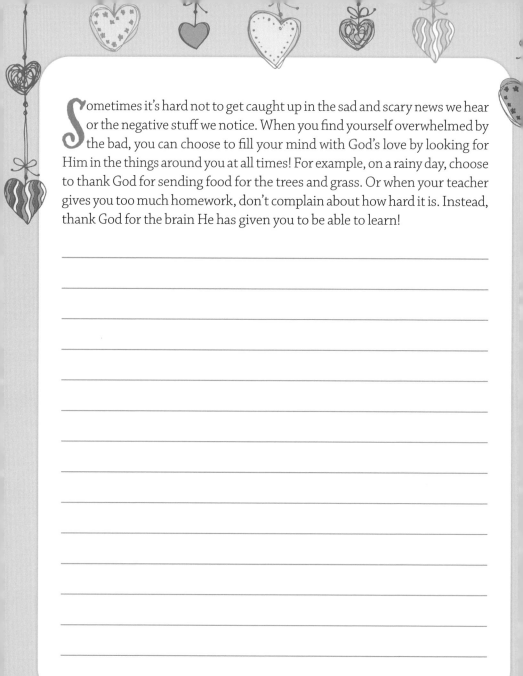

Sometimes it's hard not to get caught up in the sad and scary news we hear or the negative stuff we notice. When you find yourself overwhelmed by the bad, you can choose to fill your mind with God's love by looking for Him in the things around you at all times! For example, on a rainy day, choose to thank God for sending food for the trees and grass. Or when your teacher gives you too much homework, don't complain about how hard it is. Instead, thank God for the brain He has given you to be able to learn!

Did you know that your mind is an open door to your heart? The words you think and say to yourself turn into feelings, and those feelings get inside your heart. Mean thoughts will pop into your head, but do not let them stay! Ask God to remove them and to help you keep your mind and heart clear of bad things. This way your mind can always be focused on Him.

Dear God,

Help me to fill my mind and my heart with Your love and the things that will make me more like You. Please get rid of anything negative that might make me less like You. Thank You for reminding me that my thoughts matter. Help me to know when bad thoughts start feeling at home in my mind, and help me replace those thoughts with ones that make You smile.

In Jesus' name, amen.

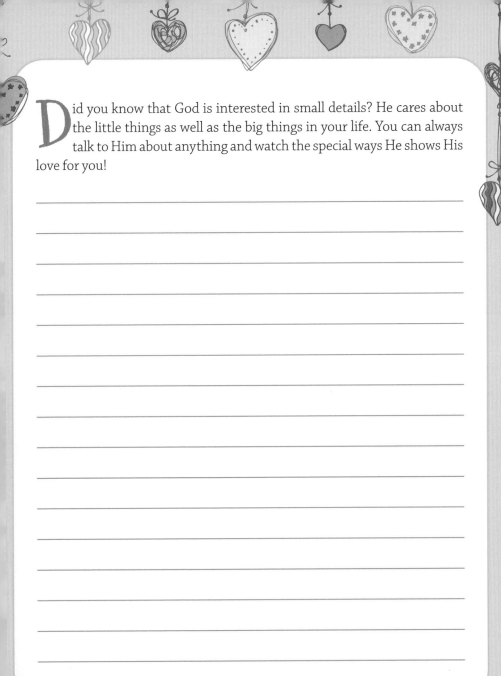

Did you know that God is interested in small details? He cares about the little things as well as the big things in your life. You can always talk to Him about anything and watch the special ways He shows His love for you!

"He said to them, 'Go into all the world and preach the gospel to all creation'" (Mark 16:15).

Choose a country (Germany, Australia, Canada, America, Uganda, China, the Bahamas...ask an adult to help you choose a country if you can't decide) and pray for the people there. Especially the girls who are just like you! Look up some information about that country, and write down that information. Pray that God will keep them safe and help them to learn more about Him.

_____

_____

_____

_____

_____

_____

_____

_____

_____

_____

_____

_____

_____

_____

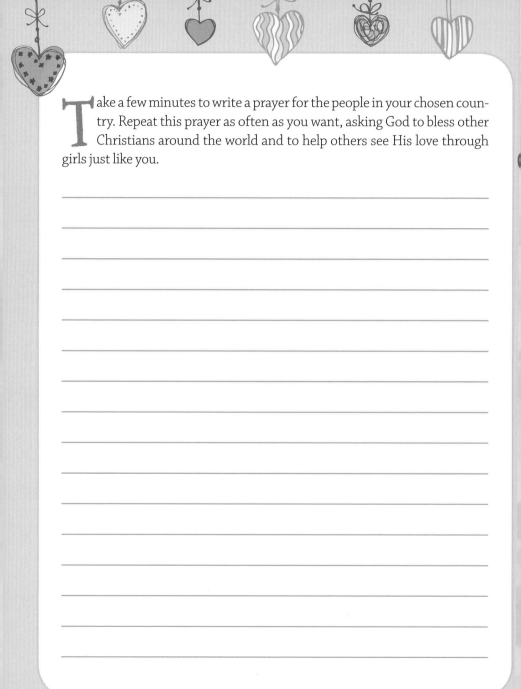

Take a few minutes to write a prayer for the people in your chosen country. Repeat this prayer as often as you want, asking God to bless other Christians around the world and to help others see His love through girls just like you.

_____

_____

_____

_____

_____

_____

_____

_____

_____

_____

_____

_____

_____

_____

_____

_____

_____

_____

Dear God,

Thank You for loving everyone. Will You help me to care about Your children around the world? Teach me to pray for them and to support them. Thank You for creating the world and all the amazing people in it!

In Jesus' name, amen.

Don't ever be afraid to talk to God when you do something wrong or to ask Him for help when you need it. Always remember that God sees you, He knows you, and He wants to help you! You can't do anything to make God love you more, but cheerfully obeying Him does bring you closer to Him. Being obedient is not always easy, but God wants to help you. Just ask Him! Pray this verse from the Psalms: "Teach me to do your will, for you are my God; may your good Spirit lead me on level ground" (Psalm 143:10).

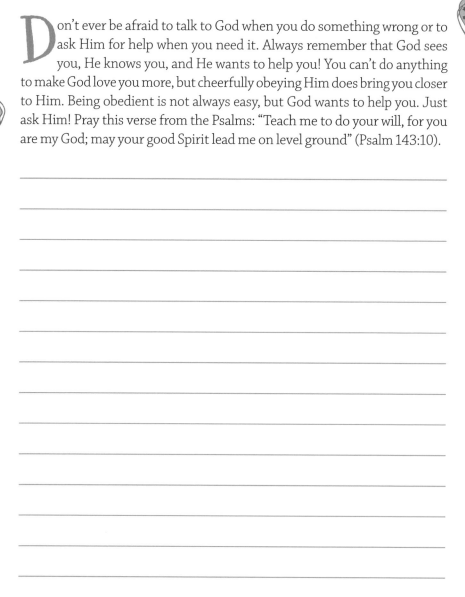

There's nothing that God loves more than when His followers listen to Him and obey His Word! What are some of the ways you can obey God today? Make a list, write a prayer, or draw a picture illustrating how you plan to obey God.

_____

_____

_____

_____

_____

_____

_____

_____

_____

_____

_____

_____

I try to listen to God and do what He tells me to do. — **Kaitlyn**

God doesn't want me fighting with my sisters. So I obey God when I don't argue with them. — **Olivia**

Dear God,

Thank You for making me a person and not a robot. I am so glad I know what it feels like to have a heart and feelings! Help me to be obedient and to know the joy that comes with loving and choosing You.

In Jesus' name, amen.

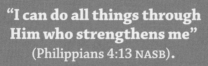

**"I can do all things through
Him who strengthens me"**
(Philippians 4:13 NASB).

When God says you can do all things, He means that no matter what happens, He will give you the strength you need to handle it. If you lose or if you win, or if you fall, fail, or mess up, God is with you and will help you move forward with your life.

_____

_____

_____

_____

_____

_____

_____

_____

_____

_____

_____

_____

Does it surprise you to know that God is with you at school while you hang out with your friends and while you are sitting in your classroom? God is even right there with you when you are home, sitting in your room, reading a book, or watching TV. The best part is, at the same time that He is with you, He is everywhere else...around the entire world.

When you know that God is with you, you can feel safer, behave better, and smile more! He is always ready to help, protect, comfort, and celebrate with you. He is even with you when you choose to ignore Him. And when needed, He is also there to correct and teach you. Your job is to accept His love and to see Him in your life every day, everywhere.

Write down a prayer, or journal your thoughts about God always being with you, no matter what is happening in your life.

Did you know that God is the best storyteller in the world? He tells so many different kinds of stories in His Word!

If you are the kind of girl who likes scientific adventures, you should start right at the beginning with Genesis. After all, God is the creator of the universe!

Do you enjoy reading about friendships? Then open up the book of Ruth and read how Ruth and Naomi became best friends during a difficult time and how nothing could destroy their friendship.

If you want to read stories about true love and risky adventure, make your way to the New Testament and open up Acts and Romans. There you will read about Paul and how his love for Jesus sent him on a journey with many twists and turns.

Have fun digging into the stories in the Bible—and learning all about God as you read!

Make a list of books you've read, books you're reading, or books you want to read. You can ask your friends or family members for book suggestions too. And don't forget, you can always include your favorite books of the Bible!

_____

_____

_____

_____

_____

_____

_____

_____

My favorite book in the Bible is Ephesians. — **Alena**

My favorite book in the Bible is Esther.
She was a brave queen. — **Kaitlyn**

My favorite book in the Bible is the
First Epistle of John (chapter 1). — **Camryn**

I like the book of Psalms in the Bible.
Especially the songs of praise. — **Olivia**

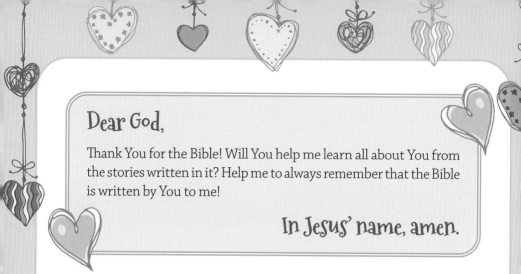

Dear God,

Thank You for the Bible! Will You help me learn all about You from the stories written in it? Help me to always remember that the Bible is written by You to me!

In Jesus' name, amen.

My Favorite Bible Verses...

There is no way for us to know what God looks like, but it is important to remember that He is not just a big idea without a face. God has a heart, and He wants you to get to know Him. The more you know about God's character, the better your relationship can be.

Write down a bunch of things you know about God. Then thank Him for everything He is!

_____

_____

_____

_____

_____

_____

_____

_____

_____

_____

_____

_____

_____

_____

W ho is in your immediate family—Mom, Dad, brothers, sisters?

What about extended family—grandparents, aunts, uncles, cousins?

Did you know that if you believe in Jesus, you're a part of God's family along with every other believer on earth? You have family everywhere—how amazing is that!

_____

_____

_____

_____

_____

_____

_____

_____

_____

_____

_____

_____

_____

_____

Dear God,

Thank You for sending Jesus so I could join Your family. I feel so special and grateful that You chose to adopt me. Never let me forget that I am Your child! Help me celebrate and show others how great it is to be a part of Your family.

In Jesus' name, amen.

As one of God's girls, you are developing so many great character qualities!
Talk to God about what you'd like Him to help you with today:

confident   pretty   smart

talented   courageous   kind   strong

blessed   happy   imaginative

truthful   successful   determined   graceful

_____

_____

_____

_____

_____

_____

_____

_____

_____

_____

_____

_____

_____

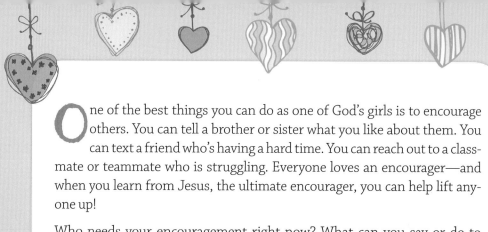

One of the best things you can do as one of God's girls is to encourage others. You can tell a brother or sister what you like about them. You can text a friend who's having a hard time. You can reach out to a classmate or teammate who is struggling. Everyone loves an encourager—and when you learn from Jesus, the ultimate encourager, you can help lift anyone up!

Who needs your encouragement right now? What can you say or do to encourage them?

_____

_____

_____

_____

_____

_____

_____

_____

_____

_____

_____

_____

Dear God,

Help me to be an encourager—a person You depend on to pick other people up from the mud. Show me those who are hurting, and give me the courage to show Your love.

In Jesus' name, amen.

_____

_____

_____

_____

_____

_____

_____

_____

_____

_____

_____

_____

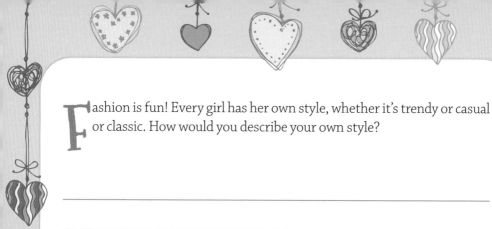

Fashion is fun! Every girl has her own style, whether it's trendy or casual or classic. How would you describe your own style?

_____

_____

_____

_____

_____

_____

_____

_____

_____

_____

_____

_____

_____

_____

_____

_____

Dear God,

Thank You for fashion and the style You have given me! Will You help me to honor You with the way I wear my clothes? Thank You that You have made me unique and special. Help me to have fun with fashion but also to focus more on others than on myself.

In Jesus' name, amen.

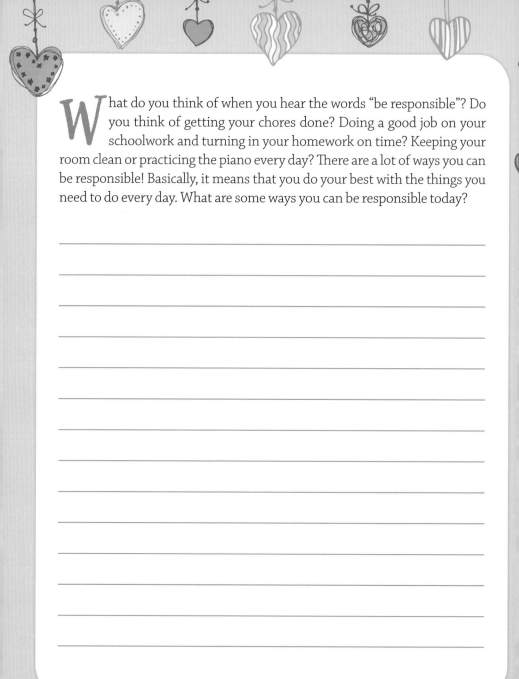

What do you think of when you hear the words "be responsible"? Do you think of getting your chores done? Doing a good job on your schoolwork and turning in your homework on time? Keeping your room clean or practicing the piano every day? There are a lot of ways you can be responsible! Basically, it means that you do your best with the things you need to do every day. What are some ways you can be responsible today?

Dear God,

Thank You for everything You've given me. Help me to take care of it all and to make good choices about how I spend my time. I want people to trust that I will do what I say I will do. Will You help me be a responsible person?

In Jesus' name, amen.

_____

_____

_____

_____

_____

_____

_____

_____

_____

_____

_____

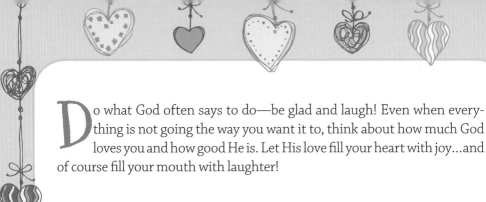

Do what God often says to do—be glad and laugh! Even when everything is not going the way you want it to, think about how much God loves you and how good He is. Let His love fill your heart with joy...and of course fill your mouth with laughter!

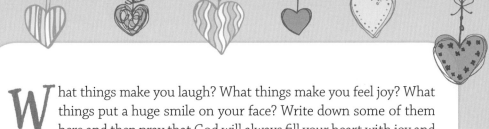

W hat things make you laugh? What things make you feel joy? What things put a huge smile on your face? Write down some of them here and then pray that God will always fill your heart with joy and gladness.

If you had a friend who wanted to come over and play only when you got a new toy or game, how would you feel? Suppose you invited them over a lot but they never came unless there was something new and cool to do. You would probably feel sad and think your friend liked you only for the things you have.

This is what it's like if you talk to God only when He gives you something new or you need His help with something. That's not what God wants. God has many blessings He wants to give you, and He loves to help you, but He wants you to love Him even when He didn't give you anything new!

> **"Love the LORD your God with all your heart and with all your soul and with all your strength"**
> (Deuteronomy 6:5).

If you ever feel like you are full of difficult emotions or feelings, take the time to talk to God about it—as well as a good friend, a parent, a pastor, or someone else you can trust. You may not want to talk about how you feel or what you are holding inside, but God can use the people around you to help you. They can help you let out some of those unpleasant feelings and emotions and help you find happiness and joy again.

Dear God,

Sometimes my heart and brain can get full of things that don't feel good. I know I can always talk to You, but I also know that sometimes I need to talk to someone else too. Will You help me talk to someone about how I am feeling? Will You help me know whom I can trust to share my feelings with?

In Jesus' name, amen.

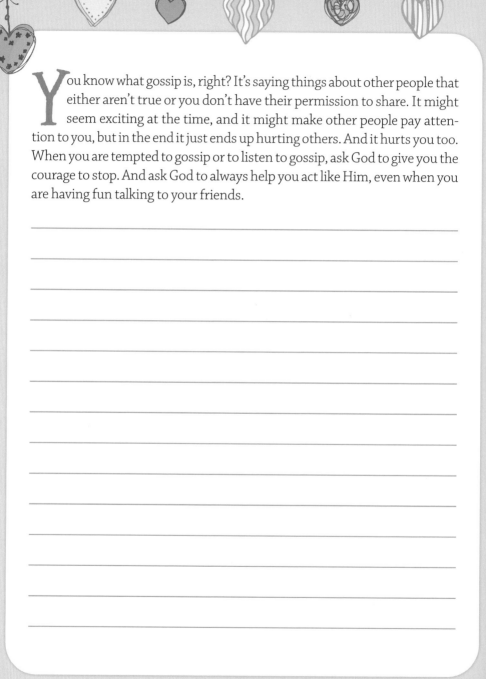

You know what gossip is, right? It's saying things about other people that either aren't true or you don't have their permission to share. It might seem exciting at the time, and it might make other people pay attention to you, but in the end it just ends up hurting others. And it hurts you too. When you are tempted to gossip or to listen to gossip, ask God to give you the courage to stop. And ask God to always help you act like Him, even when you are having fun talking to your friends.

D o you ever compare yourself to others? It's hard not to! But comparing yourself isn't a very healthy way to live your life. No matter who you are, it seems like you will always find someone else who is prettier, or richer, or smarter, or taller, or faster...you name it! So don't concentrate on what others are doing. Concentrate on being your best *you* and living your own life—the life God intended only you to live! And when you find yourself comparing yourself to others, you can pray this prayer:

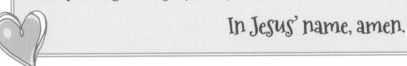

Dear God,

I know there are people who are better than me at _____ _____, but I love doing it. Help me to keep on doing it! Help me to give You glory as I try.

In Jesus' name, amen.

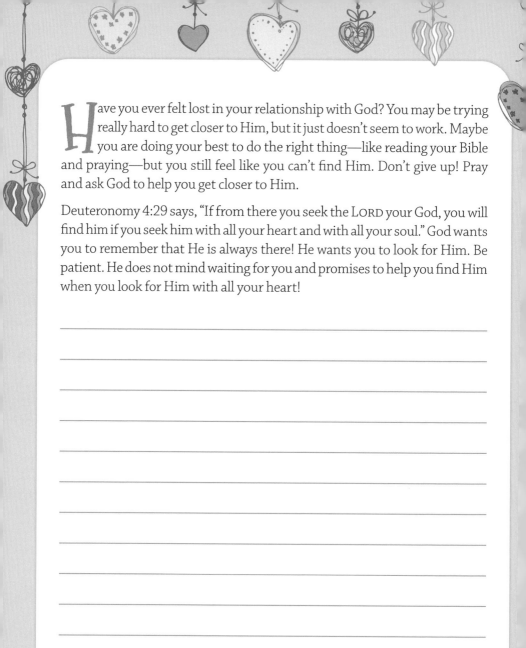

Have you ever felt lost in your relationship with God? You may be trying really hard to get closer to Him, but it just doesn't seem to work. Maybe you are doing your best to do the right thing—like reading your Bible and praying—but you still feel like you can't find Him. Don't give up! Pray and ask God to help you get closer to Him.

Deuteronomy 4:29 says, "If from there you seek the LORD your God, you will find him if you seek him with all your heart and with all your soul." God wants you to remember that He is always there! He wants you to look for Him. Be patient. He does not mind waiting for you and promises to help you find Him when you look for Him with all your heart!

Dear God,

I love You and want to know You more. I commit to looking for You with all my heart, because I know You are reaching out to me. Please help me to always remember that I am Your child. You are my identity, and I am only who You say I am!

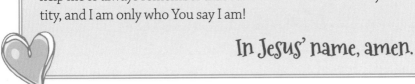

In Jesus' name, amen.

5 Daily Prayers Just for You!

Monday (Learning)

Dear God, thank You for a good weekend. Please help me at school this week. I pray that You will help me to focus. I pray that my teacher will be able to help me learn more.

Tuesday (Friendships)

Dear God, I pray that my friends will have a good day today and that You will help them to learn about You. Help me to be an example to the friends who don't know You and to be helpful to the friends who do know You.

Wednesday (Obedience)

Dear God, thank You for forgiving me of my sins. I pray that I would please You today in all I do. I also ask You to help me to be obedient to my teachers and coaches and parents and others in authority.

Thursday (Show Jesus)

Dear God, I pray that You will help me to tell people about You and Your Word so that somebody who doesn't know You will get to know You.

Friday (Thank You)

Dear God, thank You for making me, and thank You for giving me parents or somebody to take care of me. Please give me a good Friday and a good weekend.

_____

_____

_____

_____

_____

_____

_____

_____

_____

I **pray** that You will draw me to Yourself.

I **pray** that I will delight in You.

I **pray** that You will be patient with me.

I **pray** that You will provide for me.

I **pray** that You will bless me.

I **pray** that You will use me to be a blessing to others.

I **pray** that You will mature me.

I **pray** that I will show Jesus in my very being.

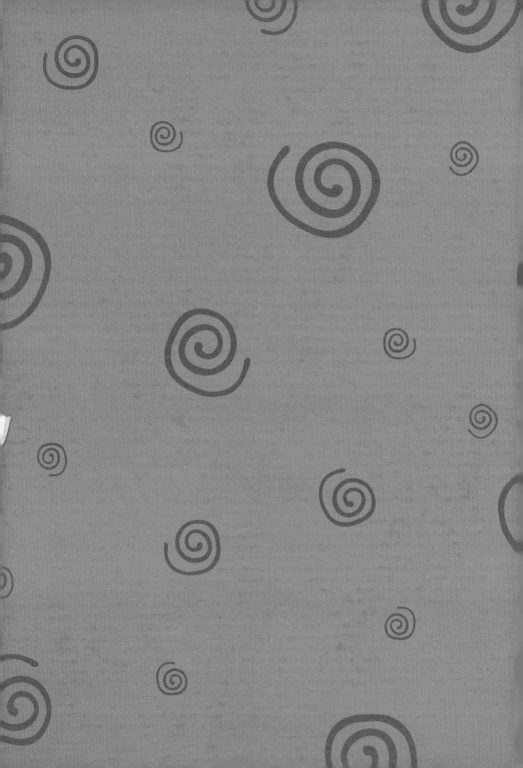